Coming to Light

Cultivating Spiritual Discernment through the Quaker Clearness Committee

Valerie Brown, JD, MA, ACC

———— Pendle Hill Pamphlet 446 ————

About the Author

Valerie Brown is an international retreat leader, writer, leadership coach, and Principal of Lead Smart Coaching, LLC, specializing in application and integration of mindfulness in daily life (www.leadsmartcoaching.com). She transformed her high-pressure career as a lawyer-lobbyist representing educational institutions and nonprofits, to human-scale work with leaders and teams to foster trustworthy and authentic connections. Valerie's books include *The Road That Teaches: Lessons in Transformation through Travel* (QuakerBridge Media, 2012) and *The Mindful School Leader: Practices to Transform Your Leadership and School* (Corwin, 2014), named one of the "best books on courage" in 2014 by the Center for Courage & Renewal. She has studied and practiced mindfulness in the Plum Village tradition since 1995 and was ordained in the Order of Interbeing by Thich Nhat Hanh in 2003. Valerie is a member of Solebury Monthly Meeting of the Religious Society of Friends (Quakers) and a certified Kundalini yoga teacher.

Acknowledgments

Valerie gratefully acknowledges the co-founders and staff of the Center for Courage & Renewal, and especially Parker J. Palmer, Terry Chadsey, and Shelly Francis. She also extends gratitude to Shirley Dodson and Carol Holmes for their work in bringing this pamphlet forward. Finally, Valerie is grateful to the many retreat participants and coaching clients she has worked with over the years whose lives serve as a powerful inspiration.

To Maya and Sophia, who are creating a life anew and to Kirsten and Karen for their ever-present love.

Publications staff: Shirley Dodson

Pamphlet edited by Carol Holmes and designed by Mary Helgesen Gabel

Cover photo by Valerie Brown

Requests for permission to quote should be addressed to:

Pendle Hill Publications, 338 Plush Mill Road, Wallingford, PA 19086–6023

Email: publications@pendlehill.org

ISBN 978-0-87574-446-9

August 2017

Coming to Light:
Cultivating Spiritual Discernment through the Quaker Clearness Committee

*"I pin my hopes to quiet processes and small circles,
in which vital and transforming events take place."*

Rufus Jones, Quaker scholar and mystic[1]

This essay explores the practice and process of the clearness committee, a means of spiritual discernment for the individual within community, as used in the Religious Society of Friends (Quakers).[2] There are several Pendle Hill pamphlets on discernment, a foundational element of the clearness committee, including *Spiritual Discernment: The Context and Goal of Clearness Committees* by Patricia Loring (1992) and *Individual Spiritual Discernment* by Jerry Knutson (2017). I was moved to write this pamphlet after observing the profound impact clearness committees had on non-Quakers in the many retreats and workshops I led where I introduced them. Quakers and non-Quakers alike can experience in a clearness committee deep spiritual discernment, transformation, connectedness, and relational trust.

The clearness committee as a means of spiritual discernment is used in two traditional ways among Quakers: for determining suitability for marriage under the care of a Friends meeting and suitability for membership in a meeting. Some groups of Quakers, largely affiliated with Friends General Conference, have taken up the use of clearness committees in nontraditional ways for personal discernment.[3]

This essay begins with my personal experience of the clearness committee, first as a member of the Religious Society of Friends and then as a retreat leader at the Center for Courage & Renewal, which uses the clearness committee as the center of its practice. I turn to a brief history of the clearness committee to give a context for its use today and then examine key elements, as I was trained to use them. I also share my personal reflections, questions, and insights in *Coming to Light Reflections.* I explore some terms and some circumstances when the clearness committee might be appropriate. I conclude the text with a sample format of a clearness committee based on my training. At the very end of the pamphlet is an appendix containing material suitable for handouts.

Throughout this essay, I use the word *God.* For me as a Quaker and a Buddhist, God is a Spirit of Oneness; the Light or Seed Within All Things; the Energy of Compassion, Love, Understanding, and Peace.

Deepening Light: My Experience of Quaker Clearness Committees

In 2005, I was married under the care of a Quaker meeting as a member of the Religious Society of Friends in a 250-year-old stone-and-cedar meetinghouse among the gently rolling hills and small farms of Bucks County, Pennsylvania. In preparation for marriage, I and my soon-to-be partner participated in a clearness committee to discern our readiness (spiritually, mentally, emotionally, financially, and relationally) for this step in our lives. The members of the committee offered great care and a generous spirit that I appreciate even more today. However, it was in a clearness committee two years later that I first understood the profound beauty and power of this intimate spiritual practice.

I was training in a two-year facilitator program at the Center for Courage & Renewal in Seattle, Washington, with Parker J. Palmer, well-known in contemporary spiritual circles and the author of many books and articles. The Center gives retreats and offers services that help people connect who they are with what they do. At the time, I was facing a crisis of vocation. I was moving slowly, with many stops and starts, from a high-pressure and unsustainable career as a lawyer-lobbyist representing educational institutions and nonprofits to work that was unclear and undefined. I sensed that training with the Center was a critical element of re-inventing my life and my work in the world.

In a tiny, highly selective cohort that received extensive mentoring from Parker and others at the Center I found an emerging sense of myself and my work as a retreat leader, leadership coach, writer, and Afro-Cuban woman.

My first opportunity to participate in a Courage & Renewal–style clearness committee was in a wooded setting in Kalamazoo, Michigan, at the Fetzer Institute. I gathered that night with Parker and four other Courage & Renewal facilitators-in-training. We met in a tiny room lit by a single white candle, with seven Adirondack chairs in a spacious circle. The empty chair was a symbol of the role and importance of silence in this process. We sat together for over two hours, sometimes in reverent silence, other times asking gently probing open questions of the focus person, who had brought a concern or dilemma to the group. Occasionally, we experienced the rhythm of the group like rough waves crashing on a deserted beach. At other times, we felt deeply entrained by Spirit as the questions took the focus person deeper into her story, her life, her soul. After the questions, after a time of mirroring back to the focus person, and after a period of affirmations and celebrations of the focus person, we felt an unforgettable sense of truthfulness and tenderness. An atmosphere of love, generosity, gratitude, and profound connectedness was tangibly present in the room. We closed as we had begun, sitting in silence, sensing a mind of oneness.

Coming to Light Reflection

I have to confess that I entered into marriage for all the wrong reasons: I was so very tired of being alone. Like many people, I held onto the fairy tale belief that I would magically fall in love, meet the right person, marry, and live happily ever after. The truth was that most of my waking day was consumed with my work life, my career as a lawyer-lobbyist, representing educational institutions and nonprofits. I chose this career because I wanted to get as far away as I could from my early life as a child, filled with violence and poverty. And so I did a lot of running. I left home at eighteen and ran from home to undergraduate school, then to graduate school, and from there to law school, and on to the bar exams, and finally I ran to the so-called dream job. The only problem with the dream job was that it was killing my soul and spirit, leaving me time-bankrupt.

As a way to deal with the pressure and stress of work, I became a closet meditator. I feared that if work colleagues learned about my spiritual life, I wouldn't be taken seriously because meditation and mindfulness were not as mainstream as they are today. I was consumed with being the hot-shot lawyer. So I did a lot of hiding and a lot of running from myself. I hid and ran for so long that I didn't really know who I was, what I stood for, what was meaningful in my life, how to share that with others, and, most tragically, how to love truly and well.

I entered the clearness committee process in preparation for marriage carrying lots of unconscious baggage. I was unprepared for marriage, for intimacy, for relationship. Recalling that night with Parker and the others, I realize that my unpreparedness for marriage was part of my

The Quaker clearness committee is a means of spiritual discernment. Spiritual discernment, about which I knew very little when I began, is the practice of recognizing and understanding God's call in your life. As a practice, discernment is enlivened by daily discipline, habits of the heart and mind, faithfulness, and commitment that help you remember and nurture your deepest spiritual intention and awaken to God's presence in and around you. Discernment is a precondition for faithful action. It is an inner faculty you cultivate over time that enables you to distinguish one choice from another and supports an honest examination of your feelings and motivations. It acts as a plumb line that helps you know when to speak in Quaker worship and when to be silent, what job to take, how to spend your money, or how to use your leisure time. In discernment, you ask yourself: "Is this of God?" And then you listen.

Discernment is the practice of being attentive, being reflective, and being loving in order to determine what is truly from God. In personal discernment about your own life, you call to mind where God has shaped your life, including where your feelings and emotions have been most engaged, and notice emerging patterns that might bring you closer to God.

The clearness committee supports individual discernment within a living community, much as spiritual direction serves to support individuals (or groups) in understanding their measure of faithfulness to a living God. Quaker faith and practice was founded on the discipline of spiritual discernment. George Fox, the best known of the founding Friends, advised, "There was the first step to peace—to stand still in the light."[4] To "stand still" in this way is not a passive act, marking time. It is an invitation to become centered and grounded in the Light. The Light reveals that which is contrary to it and gives us wisdom to act with integrity. The Light allows us to see our habits and shadows and causes us to examine how we are living. We begin to question what we consume, how we spend our time, what we read, and our relationships. As we reflect on these choices, we get a clearer picture of our lives.

As a lawyer-lobbyist, I was accustomed to muscling my way through life by sheer willpower and grit. However, as I learned to practice spiritual discernment, I understood that you don't muscle your way through saying, "Give it to me straight and give it to me now." Discernment is not a tool that you pull out of a bag for convenient use. It arises from faithfulness, unfolding over time as you cultivate your own inner spiritual landscape and relationship with God. You purposefully and intentionally practice openness, attentiveness, forgiveness, and kindness of inward and outward life and relationships. A God-centered trust develops that unfolds within you and supports clarity and integrity of action. Integrity encourages a sense of wholeness in which your values and actions align.

History of the Clearness Committee: An Overview

> *Spiritual discernment lies at the heart of Quaker spirituality*
> *and practice. It's grounded in the central Quaker conviction*
> *of the availability to every person of the experience and*
> *guidance of God, immediate as well as mediated.*
>
> Patricia Loring, *Spiritual Discernment*[5]

The Religious Society of Friends emerged as a spiritual movement in the 1640s in England during a period of political and religious upheaval when many people sought new ways to understand Christianity. People were drawn together under the leadership of George Fox and others who encouraged them to be guided by a direct encounter with the Spirit, which they understood to be Christ. They were seeking an authentic return to "primitive Christianity" as practiced by the followers of Jesus in the first century. Early Friends discerned through prayer, worship, and study of Scripture whether they were "clear" or had "clearness" about leadings or callings to action as an expression of their faith. Among many contemporary Friends, the clearness committee has developed as a way to support Friends seeking clearness in their discernment, offering a loving, supportive, and prayerful community when they are facing a challenge or decision.[6]

The clearness committee is a vital component of spiritual discernment in community in part because many Friends meetings have no minister, no outward sacraments, no water baptism, no Holy Communion, and no liturgy. Most Friends believe these liturgical observations are best experienced inwardly. Douglas Gwyn has said, "True communion with God and one another takes place at the center of our beings, as we yield to the light within."[7] In the absence of external ritual practices, Quaker communities serve as testers of the rightness of a person's sense of Spirit, leading, and depth of yielding to the Light in order to get clear.

Early on, committees of experienced members were used by Friends to ascertain the appropriateness of marriage under the care of a Quaker meeting and to consider requests for membership. These committees had specific goals. The clearness committee for marriage determined that the couple had no other relationships in place. Today, it serves as a support for the couple and discerns their readiness to marry. Similarly, in questions of membership, a clearness committee might ask if the person is a member somewhere else. In these cases, clearness has a role both for the meeting and the individual. In the mid-twentieth century, clearness committees began to expand and shift to an uncodified and flexible form that could be adapted to a variety of uses and settings, including secular settings.[8] In the twenty-first century, many Friends now use clearness committees as tools of personal discernment when facing important life decisions, such as taking a new job, adopting children, or relocating.

The purpose of a clearness committee for an individual is to help find clarity on how to proceed in the face of a dilemma. Through worship and open-ended questions, the focus person is assisted in discerning the presence of God in the concern, clarifying next steps, or considering new and unexplored options. Members of the committee are not there to offer unsolicited advice, fix, save, or counsel the focus person, but are there to help the person uncover blind spots and reflect on unconsidered factors. Even if committee members are very wise people, they are charged to listen without prejudice or judgment and with open hearts and minds, and to offer emotional support as the focus person seeks to find their own personal truth and best course of action. The underlying assumption among Friends is that each person has that of God within, has an Inner Teacher—an inner source of wisdom.

In the 1960s, Young Friends of North America (YFNA) turned to the clearness committee for discernment on issues that were "too personal or not sufficiently seasoned to bring under the weight of the meeting for business." Over time, Quakers "assimilated to the wider society with its high value on privatism and individualism." Issues that formerly might have been of concern for the meeting community became regarded as private.[9] While this privacy might not have been all bad, its downside was that it deprived individuals of community guidance and support. In the 1970s, some members of the YFNA linked to the Movement for a New Society (MNS), a network of social activists committed to the principles of nonviolence, and explored the use of the clearness committee as a secular process of decision-making. MNS coined the term *focus person* to describe the person in the clearness committee who presents the question, concern, or dilemma to the committee.[10]

As it has evolved, the clearness committee offers "a way back into community support and guidance at critical times in peoples' lives."[11] The clearness committee not only functions as an instrument of discernment, it also "helps recover the communal dimension of the spiritual life in relationships, in the vitality and authority that come of profound union in and commitment to God."[12]

While the clearness committee can be used for secular purposes, for Friends it is an individual and communal process of spiritual discernment and support, an instrument to understand the movement of God in a person's life. "We pray, listen, evaluate, sift through possibilities, and then we act. ... Discernment is not finished when we make a decision."[13] There may be no clear-cut answer at the end of a clearness committee; instead the focus person may ask deeper questions, make deeper explorations as they attempt to determine where God is leading.

For Friends, it is a lifelong and perhaps daily practice to learn how to discern whether a leading, prompting, or nudging is from God. It takes disciplined reflection to know the difference between a sense of leading and your "own contributions of thought and imagination."[14] Thoughts, emotions, reactions are all useful in weighing choices that align with Spirit-led ways.

Coming to Light Reflection

I became a lawyer before I knew who I was. I have been grateful for the decision to go into this field of work because it has enabled me to make great legislative achievements and to help many people, while having a secure income. However, there was a high price: emotionally, relationally, spiritually, and physically.

I started exploring a shift in career while I was still fully entrenched in my legal career. I decided to enroll in a single graduate course at night in holistic spirituality at Chestnut Hill College in Philadelphia. For the first few weeks of the semester I noticed I was very short-tempered, and, as the days went on, I was feeling boiling hot mad. One day, a fellow student stopped me just outside a classroom to ask a harmless question, something like directions to class, and I flew into a rage. After off-loading on her and then apologizing, I decided to sit down with myself to figure out what exactly was happening with me. As I began to reflect on my motivation to study spirituality, forgiveness and reconciliation, and Christology, I realized I was moving into a vast uncharted and unknown territory of my soul and aligning my life to something deeper. In enrolling in this program at Chestnut Hill College, I was learning, perhaps for the first time, to trust the Truth within me, to allow myself to be an instrument of God's will. Previously, I believed that if I went to law school and passed the bar exam, a good job would probably be waiting for me somewhere. In other words, I craved predictability, a sense of certainty that was lacking in my early life. I wanted external validation that I was on the right path. At Chestnut Hill, I was not following an outward trajectory or external signals but instead an inward motion, an imperative I could hardly articulate to myself—or understand.

Quakers adhere to the belief in the possibility of communion with the Divine, the Light Within, and a commitment to living lives that outwardly attest to this inward experience. The Light and the Seed Within are two of the many terms that designate the divine source and inner certainty of Quaker faith—a faith grounded in experience. *Light* and *Seed* refer to the reality for Friends of God's presence within us for our own healing and wholeness and for the healing and wholeness of others and the world. The seed image is an apt metaphor for spiritual work. Imagine a tiny seed, lying silent but stirring against its hard shell to reach into growth when the conditions are right: the right soil, right temperature, right light, and right amount of water. These conditions nurture the seed's growth from the darkness of the soil into the light. Like the seed, we need the right conditions to support our growth. Unlike the seed, we need to create these conditions—to quiet our outer busyness and silence our inner chatter, so we can open and grow.

Patricia Loring describes discernment as "a gift from God, not a personal achievement."[15] Part of the discernment process is recognizing when it is time to "wait and wait again" or to consider "whether a leading is being withdrawn."[16] Sometimes discernment may be a sense of realization without the need for any specific action. Your understanding or point of view may shift and that may be action enough. Brian Drayton and William Taber cite the example of John Woolman, an ardent eighteenth-century abolitionist from New Jersey. Woolman was sure he was called to go to the West Indies, sought to obtain clearness from his meeting, and prepared himself to leave—but then "felt the concern taken from him."[17]

For Friends, it is important to recognize and understand how attachments to expectations, hopes, assumptions, impulses, and underlying family patterns shape our sense of leading. However, a "discipline of faithfulness frees us from deep attachment to the outcomes of our leadings, and allowing ourselves to be so attached can itself make us less sensitive to guidance."[18] The process of recognizing attachments begins with choosing to pay attention to our experience of our inner lives and our environments. When we do this, we notice a mixture of light and dark, ideas and feelings, things that give joy and things that sadden. The mixture grows more complex the more we let it register in our awareness. Our thoughts and feelings, our desires, attachments, and fears, our responses to people, places, and what is happening around us are all occasions in which we create a unique relationship with Truth.

"Deep Calling Under Deep": Key Words of the Clearness Committee

"It seemed to me like deep calling under deep . . . in time the cloud gradually appeared to disperce [*sic*], till at length . . . the Clerk could form a minute recording that the Meeting sweetly united."[19] Friends have described the inward motion of discernment of the Spirit in a variety of ways. The following words are particularly relevant for the clearness committee process.

Waiting

Waiting describes a living experience that not only refers to the passage of time but also to a spiritual practice or spiritual state of receptive alertness and loving attention. Waiting, as used among Friends, is both "passive/receptive and active/responsive."[20] It is the nurtured state in which you cultivate focus while letting go of distractions. The theologian Howard Thurman says in *Meditations of the Heart* that waiting is not inactivity. He articulates the spiritual quality of waiting in these lines from a poem about centering:

> Over and over the questions beat in the waiting moment.
> As we listen, floating up through all the jangling echoes of
> our turbulence,
> there is a sound of another kind—
> A deeper note which only the stillness of the heart makes
> clear.[21]

Watchfulness

Watchfulness refers to an "inward attention on our condition, not far from the threshold of prayer" that fosters sensitivity to the "little hints and motions of the Spirit."[22]

Gathered

Gathered is a term Friends use to describe being fully present, truly listening while waiting silently with the expectation that God's presence can be discerned. It is this process of "inward recollection" that forms the basis for worshipful presence, supporting the clearness endeavor.[23]

From a Quaker perspective, to be gathered inwardly is to be centered with the mind oriented to the power of Spirit. When a clearness committee is gathered, it is centered, where "various individuals and their diverse thoughts feel that they are part of one body, drawn together by Christ."[24]

Feel or Feeling

Early on, Friends expressed their inward experience in terms of feeling. A feeling may call one to act or express a belief in a certain way. This feeling "is a kind of knowing, a moment of clarity on a specific point, a heightened or intensified awareness of a situation, condition, or fact."[25] George Fox has been described as having "a knowing without words, perhaps even a pre-conscious realization."[26] Friends also refer to *feeling clear*, meaning, in yet another sense of the word, that "one had no further obligation to continue with a task, or to feel that one has no objection to a particular course of action."[27] Or one might *feel clear to proceed*, meaning "that one is led in a spiritual sense to an action. This understanding of feeling is rooted in the Quaker experience that God's guidance can be perceived, or felt, by the individual in the course of daily life, and that one's life can be (should come to be) shaped by responding to this knowing."[28]

There are no foolproof guidelines to knowing whether to trust your feelings when seeking clarity. However, you can come to know and understand yourself, your underlying patterns, your habitual ways of thinking, your fears and distractions, your unconscious assumptions. Daily spiritual practice, such as prayer, quiet reflection, silence and stillness, rest and renewal, meditation, reading Scripture and other wisdom literature, and body-centered practices like yoga or tai chi can broaden and deepen self-awareness. This awareness allows you to become more acquainted with the voice of your Inward Teacher, with how God is working through you and through your experience.

Coming to Light Reflection

In the candlelight of that two-hour clearness committee with Parker, I felt firsthand the truth about the presence of a living God. I understood the role of the Quaker practice of expectant waiting, a kind of inward attention and watchfulness. I felt the power of silence to illuminate the darkness. I felt nourished on a very deep level that is still hard to put into words. I understood the rigor of consciously focusing my attention to let go of distractions and impulses while also inwardly sensing my own feelings, sensing the relationship within the group, and sensing the focus person.

Key Elements of the Clearness Committee

In the section that follows, I address key elements of the clearness committee, circumstances when it might be appropriate to use the clearness committee, how the spiritual practices embedded in the clearness committee—such as deep listening, expectant waiting, and inward attentiveness—support discernment, and I conclude with a sample format of a clearness committee.

✤ Every person has an Inner Teacher, an inner source of wisdom

The central tenet of the clearness committee is that each person has an Inner Teacher, a source of wisdom that offers guidance.

There are no "external authorities on life's deepest issues, not clergy or therapists or scholars; there is only the authority that lies within each of us waiting to be heard." But that inner voice can often be hard to hear because of various kinds of "inward and outward interference. The function of the Clearness Committee is not to give advice to or 'fix' people but rather to help people remove the interference so that they can discover their own wisdom. . . . If we do not believe in the reality of inner wisdom, the Clearness Committee can become an arena for manipulation. But if we respect the power of the inner teacher, the Clearness Committee can be a remarkable way to help someone name and claim his or her deepest truth."[29]

Since the clearness committee is not intended to fix the focus person, "there should be no sense of letdown if the focus person does not have his or her problems solved when the process ends. *A good clearness process does not end*—it keeps working within the focus person long after the meeting is over. The rest of us need simply to keep holding that person in the light, trusting the wisdom of their inner teacher."[30]

Double confidentiality

The clearness committee process is totally confidential, creating an emotionally safe space. When the process is over, committee members will not speak with each other or with others about what happened—and they will not speak with the focus person about the issue unless the focus person requests a conversation.[31]

Open, honest questions, not giving advice or attempts to fix things

Questions should be "authentic, challenging, open, loving questions so that the focus person can discover his or her own agenda without being burdened by the agenda of committee members."[32]

Questions should help the focus person clarify their inner truth. Questions that satisfy a committee member's curiosity are not helpful to the focus person. Asking open-ended questions may sound simple, but it is not easy, in part because we live in a quick-fix, answer-oriented society. Open questions are short, concise, and to the point. They avoid projections or analyses of the situation. They help move the focus person to new insights, new ways of thinking about a dilemma. Such questions as "Have you considered therapy?" or "Have you read ____ book to help you with this problem?" are examples of leading, closed-ended questions that verge on giving advice or problem solving.

For many people, refraining from advice is challenging because it "violates the ordinary social use of verbal interchange as an occasion for display of oneself and assertion of one's ideas" and because "our culture equates helping people with giving them something: whether material aid, ideas, or a plan of action. If we haven't 'given' something to the other person, we tend to feel we haven't really helped them."[33]

The clearness committee is highly counter-cultural. The normal rules of social engagement are suspended in the clearness committee: Committee members may ask open questions only and take notes of the question asked and the focus person's response and any direct observation of the focus person's body language. They may not make statements or offer suggestions. They should not engage the focus person in any way that might distract from a deep dialogue with the soul. For example, if the focus person becomes teary, committee members should refrain from offering a tissue or words of comfort. Conversely, if the focus person cracks a joke, committee members should not indulge in hearty laughter. This does not mean that committee members are unengaged, uncaring, unemotional, or apathetic. At first glance, this may appear inconsistent with the sense of care and goodwill at the heart of the clearness committee. Committee members are engaged in a delicate balance of neither "invading nor evading" the co-created safe space. Committee members are responsible for body language that might subtly or not so subtly, intentionally or unintentionally, send a message to the focus person. The focus person is exploring their own truth and should not be burdened with the responsibility of satisfying others' curiosity or convincing them. The focus person may wish to keep their eyes closed or look at some point in the room, a candle perhaps, so as not to be drawn into nonverbal cues. Nonverbal cues are powerful and can distract the focus person from their own internal dialogue with their soul.

The use of silence to open and close the committee, to punctuate questions, and to gently invite the process is also counter-cultural. There are people for whom silence is uncomfortable. They feel the need to speak their thoughts aloud, and this helps them clarify their viewpoints and beliefs. For others, speech is uncomfortable. Perhaps they were raised to be seen but not heard. Some live in their heads too much, thinking but not speaking what is in their hearts and minds. For everyone, honest self-reflection will be needed to find how to stay true to their temperaments while finding how to authentically speak their truth with love and respect. Silence should be viewed by all as a valued member of the committee. This silence is "an intentional return to the Center, to give over one's own firm views, to place the outcome in the hands of God, to ask for a mind and heart as truly sensitive to and accepting of nuanced intimations of God's will."[34] Clearness committee members should allow silence to flow "gracefully around questions and answers," "to allow the questions and answers to sink into … the silence," taking a posture of "attentive, prayerful listening."[35] The pace of questioning and answering should be spacious, relaxed, and gentle. Silence does not mean nothing is happening.

In receiving open questions, the focus person has several ways to respond. They may answer the question. They may decline to answer the question for any reason or no reason. They may ask that the question be re-phrased. Sometimes the focus person is not ready to respond to a question, especially if it touches a place where feelings are unassimilated, fresh, or tender. Often such a question is asked at the beginning of a clearness committee. The focus person may ask the committee to write down the question and return to it later.

During the clearness committee, members are invited not only to listen deeply and lovingly and ask open questions but also, as mentioned earlier, to take notes. These notes may include questions directed to the focus person, the focus person's responses, and observations of the focus person, such as body language or tears. Members of the committee should not editorialize when note-taking. In other words, no projections or assumptions, such as "You looked depressed when asked about your relationship with your mother." It would be better to note: "Your shoulders slumped and you looked at the ground when asked about your mother." At the end of the time allotted for the clearness committee, the notes are given to the focus person. These notes can serve as a valuable record of the focus person's soul speaking.

☙ Intuitive and nonhierarchical

The clearness committee is a process of intuitive discernment, grounded in a personal relationship with God and the conviction of the availability of Inward Guidance. To enter into the discipline of the clearness committee is to reclaim restraint of speech and sensitive, reverent listening. The process is nonhierarchical and grounded in the Quaker testimony of equality, treating everyone, everywhere, as equally precious to God, recognizing that everyone has gifts to share. The process, while a reverent

and a serious undertaking, "doesn't preclude laughter, a sense of
… celebration or joy" when appropriate.[36]

⚜ Deep listening

> *"When we listen with our heart, we allow the reality*
> *of things to touch us below our identity. When we listen*
> *below our identity, who we-are* [sic] *is in-formed (formed*
> *inwardly) by the depth and breadth of things."*
>
> Mark Nepo, *Seven Thousand Ways to Listen*[37]

Douglas V. Steere says, "To listen another's soul into a condition of disclosure and discovery may be almost the greatest service that any human being ever performs for another."[38] Steere describes the intensity of presence that is the hallmark of a clearness committee. Committee members maintain attentiveness, listening deeply and letting go of preparedness, analysis, and intellect, sinking into the silence, sinking into the open question and its answer, and waiting on whatever arises. Too often we are unprepared to listen. Our everyday listening is selective. We listen for what we expect to hear or what we hope to hear. Or we listen in a shallow, surface way, physically present, but with our mind elsewhere. Committee members do not coach or cheerlead the focus person to a goal. Rather, they turn to inward attentiveness, being fully present, gathered to seek God's will through waiting, listening, compassionate support, and understanding. This is a practice of quieting the mind and centering the body. This kind of listening is open and receptive, honoring natural pauses and deep silence, ambiguity, as well as the resonance of another, the spoken and unspoken, the energetics of the relationship. Committee members perceive whether their own interior movement is aligned with others' interior movement; they sense God palpably present.

I learned about listening the hard way and don't recommend it! I am divorced and the reason my husband gave for wanting a divorce was my inability to listen to him: the hotshot lawyer, I had the answer even before he asked the question.

However, the divorce put me on a path to understanding myself and how I listened. I realized that my listening was more like a cat getting ready to pounce. I was anxious, nearly holding my breath, waiting for the person to shut up so I could speak, counsel, give unsolicited advice, or fix the person or the problem. One of the first things I did after the divorce was take a course in active listening at the Wainwright House in Rye, New York, on the Long Island Sound. There, I learned a lot about listening. I learned to listen not just with the ears to hear, but with the eyes to see, the heart to feel, and the mind to focus.

When to Use the Clearness Committee

> *Query 27: Live adventurously. When choices arise, do you take*
> *the way that offers the fullest opportunity for the use of your gifts*
> *in the service of God and the community? Let your life speak.*
> *When decisions have to be made, are you ready to join with*
> *others in seeking clearness, asking for God's guidance?*
>
> Britain Yearly Meeting, *Quaker Faith & Practice* 1.02:27[39]

There are times when we want the support of others as we navigate life. There are stressful times when our plans have gone awry, very awry, and we find ourselves in an in-between space, caught in indecision. Too often at these times, the inclination, especially in the American rugged-individualist culture, is to go it alone. As Parker Palmer has said, too often we privatize matters of the heart, trying to think ourselves out of a box. The clearness committee is ideal for these situations. Some examples of such situations follow.

Questions about aligning "soul and role," questions of calling or vocation

My friend and colleague, the poet Caryl Ann Casbon says:

> The question so often asked of college seniors, "What are you going to do with your life?" is not a query we answer once. As a result of growth and further education, promotions, obsolescence, or emergence of untapped inner gifts, etc., at any time we can find ourselves asking the question, "What am I here to do, and am I in the right place to accomplish my vocation, to follow my calling?" On a very deep level, we understand our "aliveness" depends on the answer to this, and when we are "off-call" we can create problems for ourselves and for those we work and live with.[40]

Questions of life's meaning and purpose

The Pulitzer Prize–winning poet Mary Oliver asks a beautiful spiritual, emotional, geographical, biographical question in her poem "The Summer Day":

> Tell me, what is it you plan to do
> with your one wild and precious life?[41]

Questions of the meaning and purpose of life are both deeply personal and paradoxically universal. We each, at some point in our life, may turn to these existential questions.

Questions about forgiveness, reconciliation, or understanding in relationships

Finding how to feel loved and cared for in relationships and how to offer love and care to others can be among life's greatest challenges. Often, relationships with the people closest to us are those most in need of healing. Unresolved family wounds cut deeply and can leave generational scars. These wounds may be calling out for healing, forgiveness, and reconciliation. What is calling for forgiveness and healing in your life?

Questions on aging through the seasons of life and transitions

Life stages present opportunities to define and reassess values, expectations, objectives, and unfinished plans. We move through childhood to young adulthood, spending years becoming educated, raising a family, caring for elderly parents, and then facing our own mortality. Casbon suggests imagining a diagnosis of terminal illness and holding a "Clearness Committee regarding unfinished business, end-of-life and treatment decisions, and how you want to spend the time left to you."[42]

Questions about self-care or life-work balance

Daily life can be frenetic, driven by a nonsustainable and over-committed pace that leaves you completely exhausted. Creating a life that balances work and rest may seem daunting. What is enough? Do you place your own self-care last, and yet seek to do good for others? Do you believe that self-care is self-indulgent? These questions may be ripe for clearness committees.

A Sample Format for a Clearness Committee

"The combination of silence and open questions got me out of my well rehearsed scripts [in a way] that allowed me to say something fresh and new. I felt privileged at being heard so deeply."

Clearness committee participant

The sample format is based on my training at the Center for Courage & Renewal. To prepare for a clearness committee, participants are encouraged to develop skills that support inward reflection and awareness. This development starts with intentionally slowing down and paying attention to mental, physical, emotional, and spiritual states. Before the clearness committee forms, potential participants should cultivate daily practices, like sitting quietly, reading and reflecting on inspirational texts, resting, prayer, and being in nature. Contemplative practices lay a foundation for sharing authentically, listening receptively, honoring silence, trusting ambiguity, and cultivating honest self-awareness and awareness of others.

In the retreats I lead, I begin the clearness committee work by introducing the Touchstones, a set of guidelines designed to create safe space within groups. (I've listed them in the Appendix.) I recommend that groups offering the clearness committee begin by discussing the Touchstones and agreeing to use them to guide their interactions. This review should take thirty to ninety minutes, depending on the size of the group.

Timeline for the Clearness Committee

A group wanting to offer a clearness committee may follow this guide.
- The focus person should select four or five trusted friends or colleagues to serve as members of the committee, although someone who is relatively unknown to the focus person who brings a quality of awareness and groundedness would also be suitable.
- Once the group is formed, a timekeeper should be selected. The role of the timekeeper is to help the committee move through the process. Each section of the clearness

committee in this format is time-limited. The timekeeper helps the committee stay aware of timing but does not serve as gatekeeper. For example, if there is a strong sense that the focus person is at the edge of a breakthrough or a breakdown, the timekeeper should wait, without interrupting, trusting the unfolding of the process.

- The committee should meet in a private place of the focus person's choosing where there is little chance for interruptions. It can be either indoors or outdoors.

- Arranging the space for the clearness committee is important, but often overlooked. Many focus persons feel a sense of guilt for "taking so much time" or for "being the center of attention." Women, especially, are socially conditioned to be passive, to put themselves last, to nurture and support others. In these instances, it is especially useful to inquire about the focus person's preferences: flowers, candles, a cozy chair, pillows. These personal touches help the focus person feel acknowledged and cared for. Too often, the focus person says something like, "Don't go to any trouble for me" or "Anything is fine." Sometimes the focus person hopes the committee members will do just the opposite. Sometimes the focus person wants exactly what has been expressed: nothing much. Or the focus person may be so consumed with their dilemma that they have given little thought to location or arrangements. In these cases, attentiveness from committee members may be welcomed.

Fifteen minutes: Focus Person Presents Opening Statement

The silence is broken by the focus person when they are ready to begin. The focus person describes their issue, concern, or dilemma, and signals to the committee when they are ready for questions. The timekeeper begins keeping track of time at this point for ninety minutes of open questions.

Ninety minutes: Committee Members Ask Open Questions of the Focus Person

Committee members ask questions grounded in deep listening. They listen for what is said and unsaid. They observe body language. They listen as an act of love and generosity. They listen with full awareness to the best of their ability. They ask brief, open-ended questions and take notes. Note-taking is for the benefit of the focus person and can be helpful in the mirroring process; the purpose of notes is to recount the focus person's journey. They are not a "court record" and if taking notes is distracting, do not take them. The notes will be given to the focus person at the conclusion of the clearness committee. Remember to hold the focus person tenderly and allow silence to be a member of the group. Allow silence to do the heavy lifting.

(If the focus person wishes to leave the room, the members of the committee should pause and wait for the focus person to return. If a committee member needs to leave the room, they should do so quietly and return quietly while the clearness process continues uninterrupted.)

Ten minutes: Mirroring or More Questions?

At the last fifteen minutes of the clearness committee, the timekeeper asks the focus person whether they want committee members to mirror back what they have heard or observed, or continue asking open questions. If the focus person wants more questions, the committee members will continue asking open, gentle questions for ten minutes of the final fifteen minutes of the clearness committee. If the focus person wants mirroring, the committee members will offer mirroring. Mirroring involves reading aloud passages from the committee members' notes, or observing something about the focus person when they were speaking—for instance, "When you spoke about your son's reaction, you shifted forward and a huge smile lit up your face." Mirroring is not about offering assessments based on a committee member's intuition or hunch.

Five minutes: Affirmations and Celebrations of the Focus Person

The final five minutes of the clearness committee are devoted to celebrating and affirming the focus person. Many focus persons have said that this is the most difficult part of the clearness committee—to fully take in the truth of positive affirmations. Committee members express their sincere gratitude and appreciation for the focus person, and then give the focus person the clearness committee notes. This is not the time to discuss what a committee member might have gained personally or how the committee member was enriched by the clearness committee. This time of affirmations and celebrations should center on the focus person. An example of a positive affirmation would be: "I so admire your courage and dignity in staying in communication with your sister." An example of what *not* to do is: "I was struggling with the same issue, and I learned so much about myself from your sharing." A sense of gratitude, wonder, and care are central to offering positive affirmations. The focus person may make a concluding statement of appreciation. As a committee, allow for a time of silence together to sense what has emerged from the process. This ends the clearness committee.

It is important to adhere to the time limits and not to cut the process short because there is a period of silence or for other reasons.

Debriefing of the clearness committee is optional and may be unnecessary when in a non-retreat setting. If a group wishes to debrief, it is best to do so after waiting several hours or, better still, overnight to allow everyone to return to a sense of emotional balance. During the debriefing, turn to comments from both the focus person and committee members about their experience of the process, not about the substance of what was said in the committee. Committee members should be mindful of the guideline on double confidentiality: not only is everything spoken in the clearness committee confidential but also members of the committee are advised not to engage the focus person in discussion of the clearness committee ever again, unless the focus person invites conversation.[43]

Conclusion

The clearness committee is transformational and foundational for my work in the world as a leadership coach, writer, spiritual director, and retreat leader. I appreciate the clearness committee's emphasis on allowing way to open. I appreciate the use of silence and speech. I appreciate the care and love expressed by committee members and the edgy place of not knowing. The gathered community is an unstoppable power; it unites us. The human story is paradoxical: it is about small intimate gestures of small circles of people, speaking and listening deeply, and it is about the largeness of love. The clearness committee is, at its heart, about the mystery of personhood and of God's call in our lives. These are intertwined dynamics by which we become more fully human.

The following material comes from the Center for Courage & Renewal and may be used by Quaker meetings and individual clearness committees.

Guidelines for Asking Honest, Open Questions...

... in support of the rule "no fixing, no saving, no advising, no correcting each other"—and in support of our intention to help each other listen for inner truth...

- An honest, open question is one you cannot possibly ask while thinking, "I know the right answer to this and I sure hope you give it to me..." Thus, "Have you ever thought about seeing a therapist?" is not an honest, open question! But "What did you learn from the experience you just told us about?" is.
- Try not to get ahead of the focus person's language with your questions. "What did you mean when you said you felt sad?" is an honest, open question. "Didn't you also feel angry?" is not.
- Ask questions that are brief and to the point rather than larding them with rationales and background materials that allow you to insert your own opinions or advice.
- Ask questions that go to the person as well as the problem, questions about the inner realities of the situation as well as the outward facts.
- Ask questions aimed at helping the focus person explore his or her concern rather than satisfying your own curiosity.

- If you have an intuition that a certain question might be useful, even if it seems a bit "off the wall," trust it—once you are reasonably certain that it is an honest, open question. E.g., "What color is this issue for you, and why?"

- If you aren't sure about a particular question, sit with it for a while and wait for clarity.

- As a group, watch the pacing of the questions, allowing some silence between the last answer and the next question. Questions that come too fast may feel aggressive, cutting off the deep reflection that can help the focus person.

- If you have asked one question and heard an answer, you may feel a need to ask a follow-up question. But if you find yourself about to ask the third question in a row before anyone else has had a chance to ask one, don't!

- Avoid questions with yes-no or right-wrong answers. At the same time, remember that the best questions are often simple and straightforward.

Learning to ask honest, open questions is challenging. We may slip occasionally into old "fixing" habits and need forgiveness, from others and from ourselves. As the old saw goes, "Forgive and remember!" and try not to make that particular mistake again. It helps to continually remind ourselves that our purpose in this exercise is not to show what good problem-solvers we are, but simply to support another person in listening to his or her inner teacher.

Center for Courage & Renewal Touchstones

- ***Give and receive welcome.*** People learn best in hospitable spaces. In this circle we support each other's learning by giving and receiving hospitality.

- ***Be present as fully as possible.*** Be here with your doubts, fears and failings as well as your convictions, joys and successes, your listening as well as your speaking.
- ***What is offered in the circle is by invitation, not demand.*** This is not a "share or die" event! Do whatever your soul calls for, and know that you do it with our support. Your soul knows your needs better than we do.
- ***Speak your truth in ways that respect other people's truth.*** Our views of reality may differ, but speaking one's truth in a circle of trust does not mean interpreting, correcting or debating what others say. Speak from your center to the center of the circle, using "I" statements, trusting people to do their own sifting and winnowing.
- ***No fixing, saving, advising or correcting each other.*** This is one of the hardest guidelines for those of us who like to "help." But it is vital to welcoming the soul, to making space for the inner teacher.
- ***Learn to respond to others with honest, open questions.*** Do not respond with counsel or corrections. Using honest, open questions helps us "hear each other into deeper speech."
- ***When the going gets rough, turn to wonder.*** Turn from reaction and judgment to wonder and compassionate inquiry. Ask yourself, "I wonder why they feel/think this way?" or "I wonder what my reaction teaches me about myself?" Set aside judgment to listen to others—and to yourself—more deeply.
- ***Attend to your own inner teacher.*** We learn from others, of course. But as we explore poems, stories, questions and silence in a circle of trust, we have a special opportunity to learn from within. So pay close attention to your own reactions and responses, to your most important teacher.

- *Trust and learn from the silence.* Silence is a gift in our noisy world, and a way of knowing in itself. Treat silence as a member of the group. After someone has spoken, take time to reflect without immediately filling the space with words.
- *Observe deep confidentiality.* Safety is built when we can trust that our words and stories will remain with the people with whom we choose to share, and are not repeated to others without our permission.
- *Know that it's possible* to leave the circle with whatever it was that you needed when you arrived, and that the seeds planted here can keep growing in the days ahead. [44]

Coming to Light Queries for Individual and Group Reflection

- What are the daily disciplines and practices that help you be attentive to the "still, small voice" within?
- Describe a time in your life when you were drawn by a "true leading." What happened and what do you notice now?
- How do you remain alert to your own underlying patterns, beliefs, assumptions, expectations and how they influence you?
- What captures your attention, negatively or positively, and how does this affect you?
- If you were a focus person, what concern would you bring before God?
- What does it mean to you to be "clear"?
- Where do you feel a lack of clarity?

ENDNOTES

1   Rufus Jones in a letter to Violet Holdsworth, 1937, quoted in chapter 24.56, London Yearly Meeting, *Quaker Faith & Practice: The Book of Christian Discipline of the Yearly Meeting of the Religious Society of Friends (Quakers) in Britain*, 5th ed. (London: The Yearly Meeting of the Religious Society of Friends in Britain, 2013).

2   Much of the material in this pamphlet is based on the work of Parker J. Palmer and the Center for Courage & Renewal and is used with their permission.

3   Friends General Conference's information on clearness committees can be found here: http://www.fgcquaker.org/resources/clearness-committees-what-they-are-and-what-they-do, accessed May 18, 2017.

4   George Fox, *Journal of George Fox*, edited by John L. Nickalls (London: Religious Society of Friends, 1975), 117.

5   Patricia Loring, *Spiritual Discernment: The Context and Goal of Clearness Committees* (Wallingford, PA: Pendle Hill Pamphlet 305, 1992), 3.

6   Douglas Gwyn, *A Sustainable Life* (Philadelphia: FGC QuakerPress, 2014), xxvii. See also http://www.fgcquaker.org/explore/faqs-about-quakers, accessed May 28, 2017. See also Brian Drayton and William P. Taber Jr., *A Language for the Inward Landscape* (Philadelphia: Tract Association of Friends, 2015), 122.

7   Gwyn, *A Sustainable Life*, 19.

8   Michael Birkel, "Leadings and Discernment," in *The Oxford Handbook of Quaker Studies*, edited by Stephen W. Angell and Ben Pink Dandelion (New York: Oxford University Press, 2015).

9   Loring, *Spiritual Discernment*, 20.

10 Loring, *Spiritual Discernment*, 21.

11 Loring, *Spiritual Discernment*, 21.

12 Loring, *Spiritual Discernment*, 21.

13 Teresa A. Blythe, *50 Ways to Pray* (Nashville, TN: Abingdon Press, 2006), 17.

14 Drayton and Taber Jr., *Inner Landscape*, 95.

15 Loring, *Spiritual Discernment*, 3.

16 Drayton and Taber Jr., *Inner Landscape*, 98.

17 Drayton and Taber Jr., *Inner Landscape*, 99.

18 Drayton and Taber Jr., *Inner Landscape*, 98.

19 *Pen Pictures of London Yearly Meeting, 1789–1893. First Part* (London: Friends Historical Society, 1907) as quoted in Drayton and Taber, *Inner Landscape*, 99.

20 Drayton and Taber Jr., *Inner Landscape*, 18.

21 Howard Thurman, *Meditations of the Heart* (New York: Harper & Row, 1953), 28–29.

22 Drayton and Taber Jr., *Inner Landscape*, 22.

23 Gwyn, *A Sustainable Life*, 81.

24 Drayton and Taber Jr., *Inner Landscape*, 134.

25 Drayton and Taber Jr., *Inner Landscape*, 68.

26 Drayton and Taber Jr., *Inner Landscape*, 68.

27 Drayton and Taber Jr., *Inner Landscape*, 69.

28 Drayton and Taber Jr., *Inner Landscape*, 69.

29 Parker J. Palmer, "The Clearness Committee, A Communal Approach to Discernment" (Seattle: Center for Courage & Renewal, nd), http://www.couragerenewal.org, accessed May 28, 2017. Used here with permission of the Center for Courage & Renewal. See also Parker J. Palmer, *A Hidden Wholeness* (San Francisco: Jossey-Bass, 2004).

30 Palmer, "The Clearness Committee."

31 Palmer, "The Clearness Committee."

32 Palmer, "The Clearness Committee: A Way of Discernment," *Weavings* (July/August 1988), 37–40, as quoted in Patricia Loring, *Spiritual Discernment*, 23.

33 Loring, *Spiritual Discernment*, 23.

34 Loring, *Spiritual Discernment*, 24.

35 Loring, *Spiritual Discernment*, 25.

36 Loring, *Spiritual Discernment*, 25.

37 Mark Nepo, *Seven Thousand Ways to Listen, Staying Close to What Is Sacred* (New York: Free Press, 2012), 122.

38 Douglas V. Steere, *On Listening to Another* (New York: Harper & Brothers, 1955), 14.

39 London Yearly Meeting, "Advices and Queries," in *Quaker Faith & Practice: The Book of Christian Discipline of the Yearly Meeting of the Religious Society of Friends (Quakers) in Britain*, 5th ed. (London: The Yearly Meeting of the Religious Society of Friends in Britain, 2013).

40 Caryl Ann Casbon, "Changes and Challenges: Framing Questions for the Clearness Committee Process." Used with permission of the author.

41 Mary Oliver, "The Summer Day," in *House of Light* (Boston: Beacon Press, 1990), 60.

42 Casbon, "Changes and Challenges: Framing Questions for the Clearness Committee Process." Used with permission of the author.

43 Used with permission of the Center for Courage & Renewal, www.couragerenewal.org.

44 Used with permission of the Center for Courage & Renewal. A downloadable PDF is available here: http://www.couragerenewal.org/PDFs/CourageRenewal-CircleOfTrust-Touchstones-stones-(c)2016-web.pdf, accessed May 28, 2017.